Darren C. Demaree

8TH HOUSE PUBLISHING

8th House Publishing
Montreal, Canada

Copyright © 8th House Publishing 2020
First Edition

All rights reserved under International and Pan-American Copyright Conventions. No part of this book may be reproduced in any form or by any electronic or mechanical means, including information storage and retrieval systems, without permission in writing from the publisher, except by a reviewer, who may quote brief passages in a review.

Published worldwide by 8th House Publishing.
Front Cover Design by 8th House Publishing

ISBN 978-1-926716-60-2

Designed by 8th House Publishing.
www.8thHousePublishing.com
Set in Adobe Garamond Pro, Bitter, LD Music and Raleway.

Library and Archives Canada Cataloguing in Publication
Title: Burning it down / Darren C. Demaree.
Names: Demaree, Darren C., author.
Description: Includes index. | Poems.
Identifiers: Canadiana 20200360914 | ISBN 9781926716602 (softcover)
Classification: LCC PS3604.E56 B87 2020 | DDC 811/.6—dc23

BURNING IT DOWN

A term
& a half
of ash

plopped
down
where we

had intended
the pasta
left us

with wine
& only chicken,
left us

almost empty
& so full
of the aging

fruit that
now, now,
now

we were
stained red
people

governed
by the whitest
of old men.

Unsharpened
& willing to pierce
the sky

with our nervous
ecstasy, tonight
we turned on

all of the lights
in the house,
we faced each other

at the table
& spoke to a man
that was not there.

It didn't take long
for our animal flesh
to roll our fists

in the spilled red
wine. After that
our tongues could

only wag. Our voices
could only howl.
Nobody could sing.

We celebrated
the floodlights
of our own peril.

Nobody saw who flipped over
the bedframes. Nobody saw
who opened up the windows.

Nobody noticed when the meat
was gone. Everybody talked
with their teeth. A crowd gathered

in the yard. We were loud
enough to become vessels
& drunk enough not to care.

The neon green
lipstick was passed
slowly. We all

became brides
& grooms of this
night. I don't

remember when
the chanting
combed our hair.

Those that whispered
stayed in the corners
unadorned, protecting

their corners, pissing
in their corners, un-
willing to dance

or play with the bones
of the chicken
we had picked clean.

Around 10pm
somebody painted
a rooster

on my chest.
I don't remember
taking my shirt

off, but it was
there when
I took off

my snap-shirt
to stare at myself
in the mirror.

Oh my, did those claws
make me believe
in an early dawn.

We were supposed to get Ohio,
so we propped up Ohio
to make Ohio worth saving.

Blue-winged R, poet
& tattoo artist, let her dog
draw all over my arms

& that animal was un-
afraid of the deep buzzing
of the needle. That dog

snagged a chicken leg
& greased up my bicep
with his intentions

to make my arms
stained glass windows
that was free of any olives.

Comfortable on the edge
of the evening
where the sparrow chirps

for company
& we are much less
adult than we were before

somebody brought up
the Senator, before we toasted
to casual mutiny,

before I brought up
that he still owned a house
about twenty miles

from our local liquor store
& hell, we're out of red
& white wine anyway.

I could use a blue
box with some Crown
Royal in it I say out loud.

Without a forest,
the roads are jackstraws
& midnight bends.

Six people in the car
& all of us sweating
nobody keeps

their hand down
when I ask how many
of us have lost pieces

of ourselves to the man
that's never shown
himself to be with us.

Pain's condensation
is always a hundred
& ten proof liquor

& we need that sort
of friendship right now.
We need the windows

to be rolled down.

I do not know who paid
or if anybody paid
for the case of liquor,

but some grand bastard
bought a carton of cigarettes
as well. Fire. Fire.

Lungs like our minds,
the smoke always begins
from a necessary place.

There are so many wires in Ohio
swinging from their poles
& never reconnected. Is that

the death Ohio wants for us?
Shall we freeze? Shall we crumble?
Shall we swing with the momentum

of this political wind? I must have
kicked the seat in front of me
for a full two minutes. I said

the Senator's name one more time
& the car turned around. I said
his name a second time. I kicked again.

The world doesn't end
when we trade a tooth
for a tooth. The world

ends when we stop
singing. I shout as song.
I could give a shit

about how beautiful
I used to be. I just want
my lips to matter more.

Clouds at night, we saw the horses
before we saw the moon
& though that healed nothing

we all felt better while we watched
them breathe amidst the descending
cold. We pulled the car over

& got the gin out of the liquor box.
We hopped the fence poorly.
We thought about praying.

All fist
& no fingers,
we talked

about eating
the stars
off of our knuckles

& each horse
seemed to under-
stand exactly

what we meant.
We gave
the horses

some gin.
We took turns
singing

the songs
we wished
had been

our prom themes.
I felt the rooster
on my chest

wake up.
I embraced
the profanity.

The desire to be the horse
next to us would not end.
They were drunk, the horses

& we were drunk
with the horses. We were
of the horses then, we could

not stay with the horses long,
because somebody mentioned
the moon, somebody

remembered the Senator,
somebody frightened the drunk
horses with his name.

We followed the horses
to the creek bed, so that we could
lie down in the cool water,

so that we could pour a bottle
of scotch on the sharp shale,
so we could taste Ohio's water

the way our father's tasted it
& with the first splash the horses
abandoned us to be terribly human.

I heard the first couple start
to make love where the grass
began to become the field

& nobody got up, nobody
stopped drinking, nobody
said a word. It happened fast.

When they finished, rather
when he finished, he did so
silently. The clouds cleared

& the clouds returned.
We were the only animals
left in this hungry landscape.

When the second couple started
making love they did so loudly
& the rest of us started to work back

to the full bottles in the car. I heard
her cum from a hundred yards out.
I heard her make her cum

from two hundred yards out.
I imagined there are walls somewhere
in the world, but I couldn't see

any of them. Somebody popped
a bottle of champagne. I suppose
every 1am deserves to be uncorked.

Fighting the desire
of the blossom
to shrink as night

digs deeper
into the wandering
control, we opened

the case of beer
& sat in the car
with the music playing

loud enough
for the whole county
to hear, for the land-

owners to try
& direct the police
to the correct two-

lane highway.
I see sirens in the world,
but I see no police.

In this world
of more coin
than eyelid,

I asked out loud
again why
Ohio would elect

a Michigan lawyer
to construct
a safety-net

for our bodies?
A ball of string,
a tendon

of promises,
he's made a red
sweater for himself

out of our parachute.
He's made us other
than flight.

Still on the edge of the field, everybody drunk
    & fresh from some dream-house sex
   in a creek bed or near a creek bed

    or as a creek bed, we all listened
    to the slow music burn us deeper
than we thought it could. We felt our bodies

   rebel against the quiet. The widower
screamed. The widower ran at the horses.
  He refused to say his dead wife's name,

but we all heard her burial in the slow roll
    of the searching drums. It was good
that he went mad right then. He needed it.

    We needed to see a full release.
  We must have gone a mile to been seen
by the man that called the police on us.

How often
we act out
the play

in our heads
& then polish
the scene

so it can happen
even brighter
in real life

& when it's dark
& we want fire
for the world

to see us
our naked anger
we end up

setting
the whole county
on fire.

All of the bodies
in the car

we drove nowhere
that would want us.

All of the bodies
a heavy cloth
that should quell

all of the fires
& when it doesn't?
We drove on.

I pulled my shirt off
to hang my shirt out
of the window, my

white shirt, the shirt
that hid all of my colors,
my tattoos, the rooster

& the large Ohio poem
that is my left shoulder
& for one moment only

I let the fabric be taken
with the wind, I let it
look like a pale flag.

That was too close
to surrender for me.
I dropped it underneath

the back tires. I told
the driver to turn up
the music. I didn't look

back. I could see the police
car lights going down
the wrong gravel road.

I saw a sparrow
fly into one of the downed lines
& burst into flames.

We were all hungry after that.
We needed new smells
& a righteous table. We brought

the vodka into the Denny's
around 2am. We bought
milkshakes
& all of the fries.

Five of us were bleeding. Four
of us had already has sex.
Nobody wanted any meat.

―᳁―

I was the first one
to almost set my beard on fire.
I don't remember who gave

me the lighter while we
we shared pulls of the vodka
with the servers

at the Denny's. I know it
was my idea to roll up
a menu and stick in the bottle.

I'd seen real revolutions
begin with bottle like that
being lit to be thrown at trains.

I didn't know how fast the liquor
would catch the flame.
I didn't know M

could throw like that.
She shattered the window.
They let us finish the meal

before they called the cops.

The key to being drunk
in the back of your own car
instead of the back

of the police cruiser
is to destroy no property
to refrain from yelling

out revolutionary poetry
& since all six of us
had done both of those

things, the sirens made sense.
I almost burned down
the Denny's. Luckily,

if you keep breaking the law
it's much easier to hide
or drive your car

without the lights on.
How warm every voice
is around 3am in Ohio.

Parked behind
the entrance sign
of a manmade lake

& out of beer
& with only four
bottles of whiskey

left for six people,
the talk moved forward
to sleeping

it off for a while,
then driving home,
ending the dinner

party seven hours
& three misdemeanors
later, but nobody

could sleep, nobody
could move, the deep
-ness of ten hours

of drinking booze
& actual revelry
left us all vibrating

at our old levels.
I lit a cigarette.
I could see his face

in the smoke.

―――

You know he refused
to shake my hand once
we all say in unison.

―――

Anything that washes up
on a manmade lake
is a threat or an ending

& if you're grotesque enough
to collect such things
then you should run for office.

―⁓―

I put my hand in the distance,
in the flat moon of our lives
& I felt only Ohio's best rage.

―⁓―

All six of us got naked
to run into the water
to wash off the intention

of more fire, more fire,
the control of more fire
& the loss, glorious loss

of a fire on its own.
We all met our own echo.
Even our echoes

felt that son-of-a-bitch
that cut healthcare,
that wanted to cut

healthcare even more,
that had invited one of us
to become a widower

before they ever could pay
a mortgage should see
us glisten, should hear us

invent the new profanity
just for him. We all knew
we didn't need clothes

to burn his old house down,
so we used our shirts as towels
& we folded our pants

on the sand. We were bodies,
beautiful and open. We
shook with adrenaline.

Naked, drunk, scavenging
for revolutions
we put our shoes on

for the gravel on the two-lane
& the glass from our own
broken bottles.

We had no need to dream.
We were protagonists.
We had no need to dream.

We had a dark horizon
we knew how to paint with
the brightest of colors

& we had three bottles left
& a lighter, a death certificate
& we had no need to dream.

Beneath my head
was a whole body
that never could

crumble when I needed
it to. So, it moved
forward, with every sip

it rallied as if whiskey
could be a supper
held at 4am.

All of us, bare
& full, unaware
of our other desires,

a stumbling parade
with an idea short
of villainy, but short

of nothing else. It
would have been different
if Ohio had mountains.

We found no chariots.
We found no gradient.
We were delivered

a mile south of the Senator's
old house without our skin
showing thin at all.

The world doesn't end
because you're drunk
& naked, holding matches.

Ohio, do you love us?
We know we do this

in opposition
to your leaking heart.

The landscape
an hour short
of dawn appears

to be peeling.
Our naked bodies
were shedding

the night as well,
but we had a bottle
& a half left

& that coated us
enough to lust
for the chill

that couldn't find
us. The wet grass
came early

in the cross-section
of our we never
forgot that night.

The sun couldn't confirm
& the moon had no say
in our wedding

of whiskey
& mournful idealism
& because there was no god

present for any of our decisions
we needed to find an endnote
for our loss

& since every vote
is made publicly we knew
whose name to utter

while we walked through
the countryside, while we
planned to torch

his origin-story.
We didn't want to un-birth him,
we just wanted to make sure

that portal, if it was a portal
for evil, would be closed
forever. It all made sense

at the time. Nobody doubted
how wrong it felt. Nobody
voiced an opposition to it.

Nobody stopped drinking.
It all made sense at the time.
We had no songs left.

―――

A night that will not
end
fears only one thing.

The soft light
of before the real light
tastes like blood

unable to leave
the pond
of its creation

& that worthless
memory hung on
for months, years.

We were naked
so we walked
in the fields

slowly. We could
see the police
cruisers passing

us while they looked
for the car we parked
near the manmade

lake. They still
wanted to arrest us
for trespassing,

for busting
that Denney's window,
for being bare

& drunk,
for having sex
in front of horses?

There's no way
they knew we would
set fire to the empty

house that first
held that Senator like
fire wasn't coming

for him directly.

Six bodies become one flame
if they're active enough
at night to trick the blue

moon into thinking
it should disappear
because real light has arrived.

We brought no pages.
We brought only skin
& liquor. Fire was easy.

We all stopped to drink
when we needed to get low
enough to not be seen.

I could see his house
from my squat. We could
all see his house from the dirt

we chose to wait in. There
were bad berries there.
We ate them because they

were waiting for us to eat them.
His house was waiting for us
as well. It was empty for us

to fill with as much flame
as we could conjure. I don't
remember which one of us

said the dead woman's name
first. It became a chant. We all
cried with our teeth bared.

There was a roar
everywhere,
but the sound

was too much
to be heard,
it had to be felt,

it had to vibrate
our skins.
A church bell

from a mile away
rang out of fear.
As we approached

the house
to burn the house
we, each of us,

looked like other
animals. We felt
like the first people.

Two of the six of us
were lawyers. We didn't
let them start the fire.

―⁓―

It didn't sound like any of us
were breathing. It sounded
like we were denied breath.

We left the dirt. We crossed
the road. The good people
that lived on the same county road

were starting to stir. We were
twelve hours into drinking
& we had saved one bottle

just for this. Everyone passed
the bottle until half of it
was gone. We left it un-capped.

We put her death certificate
in the bottle. We had
no more thoughts of language.

A dog approached us.
She did not bark.
She licked the concrete

where we had spilled
the whiskey. She trotted
towards the first voice

of the new day. She never
looked back. She knew
there would be a fire

& she didn't want
to have to escape
another one of those.

I wanted to read a poem
before we lit the death
certificate, but I was overruled.

This fire had a home
in all of us,
but we had to give it up,

so that Ohio could
have more than
an abandoned house

that still echoed
with the first joys
of our most prominent

naysayer. How many times
since his childhood
had he taken pleasure

from denying our common
requests for a little life
beyond his control?

The body-count alone
demanded an ash-
offering. We obliged.

～

A truck started
a quarter mile
away. It was now
or it would always
be now, forever.

～

I could hear several people emerging
from their houses. They saw us six
naked folk with a lit bottle of whiskey

& they knew where we were standing
& all of them were waiting to see what we
might do before they told the police where

they were calling from. We looked at all
of them. Nobody got smaller. Nobody
avoided our gaze. I saw a woman

look at the sun for a full moment
& when she breathed deep enough
to give me permission I threw the bottle.

I didn't expect an explosion,
but there was an explosion.
Somebody had left

a partially torn-down meth setup
in the kitchen of the house,
so that fucker went up

like we had dropped a bomb on it.
We couldn't disappear after that.
We were on our asses after that.

Everybody with a camera phone
finished taking our pictures while
we waited for the police.

We stank from the effort. I wanted
to smell like a fire, but I didn't.
I smelled like a long, beautiful night

that ended with an ending
that could never wash off. I fidgeted
a little in the first rising dust

of the day. I watched the flames
& thought of the horses
from the creek. They would have

been so proud of us right now.
I thought of my friend's dead wife.
I fell asleep on that road

& I dreamed of no terror
& I dreamed up until they cuffed me
& reminded me of my many rights.

The best part
was that the rooster
on my chest

held the table
of the police
officer's eyes long

enough to get
her to question every
part of our night.

The best part was the house
made the news that night
& the Senator had to answer questions

for a week about why six people
with no records got drunk
& naked & blew up his house.

Why the explosion to end
the world? He didn't own
the house anymore, but the meth

that was being cooked there
he had to answer for that as well.

The best part was he had to say
her name out loud on television.
We got bailed out of jail quickly enough

to pick up breakfast three days later
& see him struggle to say her name
& though that did nothing to bring her

back to life, it felt like she had been
carried a little bit further
into the bosom of a real Ohio.

ABOUT THE AUTHOR

DARREN C. DEMAREE is the recipient of a 2018 *Ohio Arts Council Individual Excellence Award*, the *Louise Bogan Award* from *Trio House Press*, and the *Nancy Dew Taylor Award* from *Emrys Journal*. He is the Managing Editor of the Best of the Net Anthology and Ovenbird Poetry. He is currently living in Columbus, Ohio with his wife and children.

A SELECTION OF OTHER POETRY TITLES BY 8TH HOUSE PUBLISHING

MANY FULL HANDS APPLAUDING INELEGANTLY

by Darren C. Demaree

5.25 x 8.5 | 194 pages | ISBN 978-1-926716-41-1 (pbk.) | $19.88

Darren C. Demaree's *Many Full Hands Applauding Inelegantly* is as masterful as it is subtle. In this latest collection, Demaree continues to expand and develop not only his power and voice, but the voice of a time and a generation. A transcendent unity runs through this tripartite collection of poems that can be taken individually, as particles or a moment on a continuous wave. Birth (A Violent Sound in Almost Every Place), Life (We are Arrows) and Death (All the Birds Are Leaving) are woven together on the circle that surrounds and unites all.

MAVOR's BONES by Rolli (Charles Anderson)

5 x 8 | 121 pages. ISBN 978-1-926716-30-5 (pbk.) | $15.88

Charles Anderson (Rolli) does it again. In another clever, witty and touching collection, Rolli rollicks again through gardens and cemeteries peopled with dreams, goddesses, characters dead and alive, dukes stricken within gout, gracious skeletons and morose angels.

"I have been dreaming / those dreams of meaning / that come from the waters / of dreaming deep / like drowned men / to the gold skin / of the ocean"

Company's come. In a ramshackle mansion, meet a family in the same condition—ancient, decayed. There's the brooding Duke, and his riotous brother. There's Grandam, lost in wilds of herself. There's a vicar, a philosopher, an angel, a ghost or two. And somewhere above them all, in a ruined garret…

"By turns delightfully black, singingly lyrical and/or innocently nonsensical. Here is a poet outside the mainstream with his own refreshingly original voice and bone[s] to pick." – Gillian Harding-Russell

PLUM STUFF by Rolli (Charles Anderson)

With illustrations by the author. Colour. 5.5 x 8.5. 128 pages. $18.88

Literate. Illiterate. Bewitching…. In his debut collection—a nine part whimsical discourse—Canadian author/artist Rolli waxes poetic about everything under "the muscular sun." There are poems about peaches and plums, about desperate celebs and monster poets, mistresses and mummified cats. Strange, celebratory, self-mocking, these are poems to be gulped down like summer fruit.

Rollick with Rolli through coddled lawns and parlour rooms, sloshing tea with gingercats under bluebird moons and slopping wine with bathing bachelorette hieresses in a world plum-stuffed with all things epicurean and bewitching, from English to Egyptian, the pathologic and the philosophic. By Canada's Charles Anderson (Rolli), recipient of the 2007 John Kenneth Galbraith Literary Award; and winner of the 2008 Commonwealth Short Story Competition.

KOLKATA DREAMS by K. Gandhar Chakravarty
88 pages, Colour, Illustrated. 5.5 x 8.5. ISBN 978-0-9809108-7-2. $18.88

Kolkata Dreams is a work of travel poetry that will transport you across the sea to northeastern India. The poems explore the idealization of Mother India against the realities of its westernization from the perspective of a Canadian-born Indo-North American discovering his heritage for the first time. When reading and reciting this poetry (you may be forced to voice these poems aloud), you will find that laughter often chokes itself on tears while the book yo-yos between meditation and contemplation. The experimental use of a first-person/third-person singular-detached narrator encapsulates the feeling of disembodiment often felt by the voyager, especially in this case, as the poet simultaneously belongs to yet remains apart from the cultures he explores. In short, Kolkata Dreams is a must-read for anyone interested in the balance between tradition and modernity, particularly in the context of globalization and twenty-first century India.

HYPODROME - Selected Poems by Jason Price Everett
148 pages. ISBN 978-1-926716-12-1 $18.88

"Begin anywhere. Stop anywhere. Everything that can possibly be written now is a drop of rain upon its vast syncretic ocean... This future of our shared media Byzantium is obscenely bright."

Jason Price Everett's poetry explodes from the page with the raucous power of industrial machinery and strikes its targets with the rapier's fine point. Honing in on the chaos of the past two decades, Hypodrome charts the growth of today's artist searching for the defining aesthetic of our time. These poems document the plastic, the losses, the frustrations and the triumphs accumulated during the course of an accelerated era, set against the backdrop of an ominously beautiful future.

MAPLE VEDAS by K. Gandhar Chakravarty
Colour with Original Artwork | 6 x 9 | 78 pages | ISBN 978-1-926716-05-3 | $18.88

The latest in a long line of scriptures, MAPLE VEDAS explores the voyages of the Gods of India – Vishnu, Shiva, Ganesha, Kali – as they visit the northwestern lands of the globe in the past, the present, and the near future. Peopled with other characters like a prophetic moose, a secretive walrus, and a charming groundhog, the interactions and dialogues of this third millenium testament force you to rethink history, religion, and your place in all of it – wherever you come from. In Maple Vedas, we discover that the Gods of India continue to roam Canada and the United States – perhaps standing beside you on a city bus – but they have come in new incarnations. Will you recognize them?

A DIRT ROAD HANGS FROM THE SKY by Claudia Serea
5 x 8. 130 pages, ISBN 978-1-926716-24-4 . $14.88

Beautiful, moving and brave; Claudia Serea's poems tell a story of fear and repression, but also one of hope. This strong collection speaks out against systems of repression all over the world, with a message that is vital and a powerful voice.

Written in unsparing, haunting detail, Claudia Serea's unforgettable A Dirt Road Hangs From the Sky brings to life the horrors of the brutal Communist repression in her native Romania in the second part of the 20th century – the prisons, the torture, the barbarous inhumanity – preserving in memory a time that should never be forgotten. She writes: "Tell me, grandma, everything you know / so I can be your mouth when you are gone." The grief is lasting; memory must serve as justice.

– Charles Rammelkamp, editor of *The Potomac Review*, author of *Fusen Bakudan*

NOT FOR ART NOR PRAYER by Darren C. Demaree
5. 5 x 8.5 | 90 pages | ISBN 978-1-926716-35-0 (pbk.) | $15.88

"...these poems gallop & salivate, these poems roar through their quiet deftness on the page. Congratulations for picking up this book, you're in for quite a ride." —Sam Sax, author of "sad boy / detective"

"...artful and prayerful..." "...these generously attentive and marvelously whimsical poems repeatedly resist sleight-ofhand poetic transubstantiation, while slyly acknowledging the inevitably transformative nature of language." —Lee Ann Roripaugh, Author of Dandarians

AS WE REFER TO OUR BODIES by Darren C. Demaree
5 x 8 . 90 pages. ISBN 978-1-926716-16-9 $15.88

Our bodies, our individual and collective bodies, and the separate bodies that together combine to make our systems, ecological, biological, psychological and technological—these are the bodies that we refer to, these are the bodies that Darren C. Demaree has dance for us on the page; nuanced or naked, dissected, desecrated and decorated; these are the bodies that rise and swell to the touch of the poet's pen.

"...a dangerous dreamer..." "unsettling in necessary ways." — Christopher Michel, Author, Editor

www.ingramcontent.com/pod-product-compliance
Lightning Source LLC
Chambersburg PA
CBHW051703040426
42446CB00009B/1278